June 9 1983
Dearest Mother
You have seen us through
Many years and Continue
to give of yourself too Much
My Wish on this day is for
You to be without Pain
Relax and enjoy life Without
So Much Work.
Your
Loving Daughter
Louise

DEAR
MOTHER

DEAR MOTHER

Words of Thanks
and
Thoughts of Love

Selected by Jayne Bowman

THE C. R. GIBSON COMPANY
NORWALK, CONNECTICUT

WHEN GOD
THOUGHT OF MOTHER

When God thought of mother,
He must have laughed with satisfaction,
and framed it quickly —
so rich, so deep, so divine,
so full of soul, power, and beauty,
was the conception.

HENRY WARD BEECHER

FIRST MOTHER

The Lord God walked in the morning cool
When the earth was a new green ball,
And He said: I shall make her beautiful
This woman to watch over all.

The brooding strength of the hills he bound
To the budding girth of a tree,
And into the golden dust of the ground
He breathed bright ecstasy.

And the woman walked in the morning cool
A heartless thing and vain;
And the Lord God said: She is beautiful,
But she lacks the grace of pain.

Then a moaning forced her lips apart,
While ministering angels smiled,
And into her body came a heart,
And into her arms a child.

VIVIEN YEISER LARAMORE

And she brought forth her firstborn son, and wrapped
him in swaddling clothes, and laid him in a manger.

LUKE 2: 7

THE PICTURE

The painter has with his brush transferred the
    landscape to the canvas
with such fidelity that the trees and grasses seem
    almost real;
he has made even the face of a maiden seem
    instinct with life,
but there is one picture so beautiful
that no painter has ever been able perfectly to
    reproduce it,
and that is the picture of the mother holding in
    her arms her babe.

WILLIAM JENNINGS BRYAN

THE MAID-SERVANT
AT THE INN

"It's queer," she said; "I see the light
   As plain as I beheld it then,
All silver-like and calm and bright —
   We've not had stars like that again!

"And she was such a gentle thing
   To birth a baby in the cold.
The barn was dark and frightening —
   This new one's better than the old.

"I mind my eyes were full of tears,
For I was young, and quick distressed,
   But she was less than me in years
   That held a son against her breast.

"I never saw a sweeter child —
   The little one, the darling one! —
I mind I told her, when he smiled
You'd know he was his mother's son.

"It's queer that I should see them so —
   The time they came to Bethlehem
   Was more than thirty years ago;
I've prayed that all is well with them."

DOROTHY PARKER

MY HEART
STARTED SINGING

The popular motion picture, "The Sound of Music," was based on the autobiography of Maria Augusta Trapp, The Story of the Trapp Family Singers. *In this excerpt, Maria, the mother of ten children, describes the arrival of the youngest member of the famous family.*

Oh, time and again (I was told) that one *had* to *have* a doctor and one *had* to go to a hospital to have a baby. I was finally persuaded to make one concession: the doctor. But go to a hospital — that was ridiculous. Why? What for? I wasn't sick. In Europe you went to a hospital when you were dangerously sick, and many people died there, but babies were born at home. Would they in the hospital allow my husband to sit at my bedside? Could I hold his hand, look into his eyes? Could my family be in the next room, singing and praying? The answer to all these questions was "no."

All right, that settled it. I tried to explain that a baby had to be born *into* a home, received by loving hands, not into a hospital, surrounded by ghostly looking doctors and masked nurses, into the atmosphere of sterilizers and antiseptics. That's why I would ask the doctor to come to our house. But I had to find the doctor first. I tried many, but each time I mentioned the word "at home," they didn't want to take the case.

When I was very tired and discouraged, I found a young doctor in our neighborhood, young and a little nervous about the whole idea, but he said he would come. I consoled him.

"Don't worry. There is nothing wrong, I know all about it. It is the most natural thing in the world. You just have to sit in the next room, and I'll call you when I need you."

His eyes widened, and he opened his mouth to speak, but closed it again in utter amazement.

And so it happened. The evening came when I knew it was time. Everything went the old way. The family gathered in the living room, reciting the rosary aloud. Then they sang hymns. Then they prayed again. The doors were open, and I could hear them. Georg was there next to me, and his good, firm hands patted me once in a while, as he repeated: "Soon she will be here, our Barbara," and then we both smiled. The doctor had not come yet. Then it had to be: "Call him now and tell him to be quick."

When he arrived, he looked troubled. He had a nurse with him — a sweet-looking young girl. They were washing their hands when all of a sudden I had to squeeze Georg's hand very hard, and time seemed to stand still. Then I heard a funny little squeak. The doctor, pale, beads of perspiration on his forehead, turned to me and said — I couldn't understand what — and then carried something in his right hand through the room. It was all over. At that minute a full chorale downstairs started: "Now thank we all our God!"

The doctor, in the middle of the room, turned around.

"What's that?" he gasped.

And then I saw what he was holding: my precious baby — head down! My heart almost stopped. I was sure he would drop her.

"Watch out — don't break her!" I cried.

"Her! Why — it's a boy!" he said reproachfully.

What? I must have misunderstood. Georg bent over me.

"Barbara is a boy," he smiled.

My heart started singing: "Now thank we all our God!"

NEW MOTHER'S SONG

My darling, don't cry
Because you've been born.
You'll see hummingbirds fly
In this world that you scorn
So vociferously now.
You'll touch tiny oak leaves
As soft on the bough
As your palm that receives
These kisses of mine.
You'll see mountains and rain
And smell cedar and pine —
Oh, my small, don't complain,
For I tell you most true
And my honor I'm giving
Any world that holds you
Is a good world for living.

JANE MERCHANT

NEW MOTHER

I need not seek or pray, my newly born,
To love you always; that is a garment worn
Without effort, one I could not put away
Even if I would. My love will stay.
But wisdom, but the gleaming instruments
Of straight perception and intelligence
To guide you when you turn to me — ah, these
Are not so readily come by! There is ease
For the heart in loving you, and not a task.
But more is required of the mind; the years will ask
For knowledge, and for skill with honesty's bright
Scalpel. It is for these I pray tonight.

ANITA LAURIE CUSHING

THERE IS
NO SUBSTITUTE
FOR LOVE

. . . During the worst of the famine in Holland, in the last winter of the Second World War, the supreme command of the German army of occupation allowed two bargeloads of babies less than a year old to leave the city of Amsterdam for hospitals in Friesland across the Zuider Zee, where food was more plentiful and where they would be looked after by a professional staff.

The barges sailed in bad weather; one of them was blown off course and ran aground on the beach near a fishing village north of the city. The babies were in a pitiable state of hunger, seasickness, and sheer terror. The fishermen of the village waded out to the ship and formed a human chain to pass them to the shore, where they were taken over by the women. That night, every woman in the village, young, old, single, married, or widowed, had a baby to look after.

A few days later, the barge was refloated and entered the harbor to take on its load of babies once more. But the women refused to give them up; despite the dire threats from nervous officials, not one child was delivered on the quayside. The barge returned empty to Amsterdam.

In each barge there had been two hundred children; of the ones who ended up in the hospitals across the water, where they were well nourished and looked after by shifts of professional nurses, one quarter died; yet all the babies taken in by the women of the fishing village survived, despite the fact that their rations were far inferior and that there was no professional help available.

There is no substitute for the life-giving comfort and warmth of being hugged, nuzzled, and loved by one motherly woman.

JAN DE HARTOG

You show a baby you love him a hundred times a day. You don't have to put it in words or even make an effort — in fact it's more real without the effort. It just comes through the nearness, through the hands, the tone of voice, the smiling mouth, the eyes.

DR. BENJAMIN SPOCK

CRADLE SONG

The winds are whispering over the sea,
And the waves are listening smilingly, —
They are telling tales of the shining sky,
And the dusky lands they travel by.
They are telling tales they have often told —
Of faces new and feelings old,
Of hope and fear, and love and hate,
Of birth and death and human fate,
Of homes of joy and hearts of pain,
Of storm and strife, and peace again,
Of age and youth, of man and maid,
And of baby mine in a cradle laid.
    And the sun laughs down in his own kind way,
For the heart of the sun is as young as they;
And the sea looks up as a loved one should, —
They are old; they know it is good, all good.
You may feel the waves as the cradle swings,
And the air is stirred with the wind's soft wings,
And mother has heard from the sky and the sea
That they send "sweet sleep and dreams" to thee
Then hush! my baby, gently rest
In the night's wide arms, on the earth's broad breast,
The sky above, beneath, the sea,
And a greater than all to shelter thee.

MERLE ST. CROIX WRIGHT

A SMALL DAUGHTER WALKING OUTDOORS

Easy, wind!
Go softly here!
She is small
And very dear.

She is young
And cannot say
Words to chase
The wind away.

She is new
To walking, so
Wind, be kind
And gently blow

On her ruffled head,
On grass and clover.
Easy, wind . . .
She'll tumble over!

FRANCES FROST

MOTHER AND
HER SECRET

You hear a lot about kids fooling their mothers, but you hardly ever hear of a mother fooling her kids. But I knew one who did. Mine. But in the end we found out the truth about her.

We grew up during the Depression. Now kids today may not know what a depression means. It doesn't mean one car in the family and steak once a week, even if that is as ghastly a life as kids today can imagine. The Depression meant no shoes, no meat and barely enough shelter — with a fighting chance that the whole family would be evicted onto the sidewalk. That was the Depression. And it was harder still because our father had left us.

Well, all through those grim years my mother managed to keep her four children fed, sheltered, clothed, and in school. Her hair turned white before she was 35. She was cheerful enough, but her eyes had a sort of haunted look. She never had any pretty clothes or good times.

When we four kids grew up, we all did well enough to pool a fairly handsome hunk of cash to send Mom each week, so that whatever years she had left from about 50 on would be different from the years before. But we were all kind of disappointed in Mom's new life. She didn't move into a new home; she said she was perfectly comfortable in the old one. She didn't hire any help to take her off her feet; she said she liked doing housework. She didn't buy any pretty clothes. She kept delaying the vacations to Florida or to Europe that we planned for her — until we gave up planning. Still, that weekly check came in, and, as we four figured it, since she didn't spend more than a fraction of it each week she must have saved a considerable amount by the time she died, some 20 years later.

Well, when we went through her papers we found that Mom was broke! Those checks had been spent the instant they arrived. On what? As soon as we kids were off her back, Mom had secretly arranged with a refugee outfit to ship her four war orphans from Europe. She'd set them up in a home near hers, and for 20 years she'd educated them, seen them through sickness and teen-age problems, and, in two cases, into marriage.

She never told us about the four new kids. I guess she wasn't sure we'd approve of her going through the whole mess all over again. I'm not sure we would have, either. You see, it isn't easy for kids who've grown up seeing their mothers knock themselves out half their lives to raise them to understand that motherhood is a sort of incurable condition.

AL CAPP

Having a large family is a more interesting experience than any other that I know and it ought to be viewed that way. It's quite a challenge.

ROSE KENNEDY

FAVORITE CHILD

Since, up to now, my greatest claim to fame
    Is children — though I've only half a dozen —
I'm sometimes asked one question, and the same
    By well-intentioned friend or aunt or cousin:
"Surely, among so many, there is one
    You love a little better than the others?
A sweeter daughter or a sturdier son?
    Hasn't it always been that way with mothers?"

Well, if you ask me, then I'm forced to say
    I have a special feeling for the first —
Because he's first; because he has a way
    Of reading and becoming so immersed
He might as well be somewhere else as here.
    Then there's the second, and I must admit
This daughter is particularly dear —
    For laughing eyes, for quick and sparkling wit.
Then there's the third, who has a special place
    Within my heart; I love her eager mind,
Her clever hands. And then I must confess
    A special fondness for the fourth, I find —
His strength, his willingness, his Jovian laughter.
    As for the fifth — ah, she's my favorite too —
For changing mood and soaring fancy. After
    The fifth, there's still another daughter who

Is favorite, being last, and being small,
  And being she. Yes, it is plain to see
Which of my children I love best of all.
  It's something no one needs to ask of me.

LOUISE OWEN

Mother is the name for God in the lips and hearts of little children.

W. M. THACKERAY

THE BIG SURPRISE

The door bangs and he rushes in from kindergarten, your rosey-nosed, cowlicky beginner, with his shirttail out and one pant leg trailing. "Mother, Mother!" He hunts you down and hurls himself against you, smelling of paste and crayons and little boy. "I got something for you — don't look, don't look."

Frantically he hides it behind his back and squirms away, eyes shining. "It's something we made at school. It's a surprise."

"A surprise? Oh, my goodness, give it to me quick."

"Wellll — it's for a special day, but it isn't that day yet."

"Dear me, well then I guess I'll have to wait."

You feel his eager anxiety wrestling with the problem. Plainly, he can't bear it. "Oh, no, I *think* it's all right to give it to you early. The teacher didn't say. But first you have to guess. It starts with V," he helpfully confides.

"V — V — oh, dear, there aren't many words that start with V. This will be hard. Vinegar — velocipede —"

"I'll give you another hint." He is ecstatic with his superior knowledge, vaguely sorry for you. "Val — val — come, try."

"Valance — valuable — I'm afraid I'm stuck."

"Give up? Give up? Here, I'll give it to you anyway." Triumphantly he thrusts it at you, the lopsided red heart with its lace paper doily trimming. "It's a *Valentine*."

"Why, it's beautiful, darling. And you made it all yourself?"

"Well, the teacher helped us just a little, but it's my very best coloring and printing." He heaves a long, proud, rather wistful sigh. "It's fun being big enough to make something for somebody, especially when they like it and are *really* surprised!"

MARJORIE HOLMES

MOTHER'S SONG

When the voices of children are heard on the green
And laughing is heard on the hill,
My heart is at rest within my breast
And everything else is still.

'Then come home, my children, the sun is gone down
And the dews of night arise;
Come, come, leave off play, and let us away
Till the morning appears in the skies.'

'No, no, let us play, for it is yet day
And we cannot go to sleep;
Besides in the sky the little birds fly
And the hills are all cover'd with sheep.'

'Well, well, go and play till the light fades away
And then go home to bed.'
The little ones leaped and shouted and laughed
And all the hills echoed.

WILLIAM BLAKE

WE CANNOT
MEASURE LOVE

Deborah Kerr writes movingly of the day her young daughter discovered the full meaning of numbers and, more importantly, love.

My daughter Francesca was about four years old when she first became aware that numbers were not just new words in her vocabulary or names of digits, but that they can be useful to express quantity. This step, as all parents learn, follows the "so big" stage.

One memorable day, Francesca turned to me to express her love with the help of her new-found knowledge and said, "Mummy, I love you ten times," followed by deep thought and "I love you twenty times."

After another short pause, she reached a breathless pinnacle with "I love you six hundred times."

A grateful hug and kiss from me produced a tiny frown and more concentrated thought which disappeared in a sigh of relief in her final outburst, "Mummy, I love you outside the line of the numbers."

My child's words touched me so deeply that I have never forgotten a moment of that scene, or the wisdom of her sudden discovery that you cannot measure love!

The insight that children "discover" never ceases to amaze me. Somehow their minds, uncluttered by the tensions of responsibility, can reach directly into the heart of a problem and make it brilliantly clear.

A knowledge that love is immeasurable is actually very subtle. And yet my four-year-old understood it completely, without the mechanics of logic — with only the instinct of the young. That day, that moment, my daughter knew what adults so often forget: we can neither demand nor give a love that can be counted or measured. We cannot measure love — and should not. But we can accept it, cherish it, nurture it, and thank the Lord for it.

HEY, MOM!

"Hey, Mom! The sky bowl spilled today
And all the blue poured on the sea!"
Thus, with one young, perceptive thought,
He gave a summer day to me.

"Hey, Mom! God whipped the clouds to cream
And made them stand in little peaks.
I wish that I could reach and taste!"
Oh, lovely are the words he speaks!

One day he held a butterfly,
Then showed me gold dust from its wings.
The touch of Time will brush away
The miracle of simple things.

My son, when you will have outgrown
The wonder of a world so new,
I pray that you will have a child,
For he will teach it back — to you.

BEULAH FENDERSON SMITH

THE LETTERS

The neighbors couldn't understand, somehow,
That, though alone, she was not lonely now.
Nice folk, the neighbors, if they'd let her be;
But they blamed her boy for going off to sea.
They scorned the lovely gifts he sent:
That shiny string of bright-pink pearls from Ghent,
The yellow crepe-de-chine shawl from Shanghai
(That was the time she couldn't help but cry),
The fan with painted roses from Peking —
Strange how Miz Collins' well-meant words should sting:
"All I can say is, ain't that like a man,
Here you are freezin' and he sends a fan!
Here when food and clothing are cruel needs,
He only thinks to send a shawl and beads;
Here when you sit alone these long, cold nights,
He thinks he's done his duty if he writes!"

But they didn't see the letters that he wrote —
Letters from foreign ports or from the boat,
Telling of all the strange things that he saw,
Wonderful letters starting, "Dearest Ma,"
Letters that all said: "Someday you and me
Will have a small white cottage near the sea."
Reading these words by lamplight, that was how
She was alone but never lonely now.
And some nights when she'd just received a note,
She'd clasp the bright-pink pearls around her throat,

Put on the lovely yellow silken shawl,
And take the painted fan down from the wall,
Then stand at the old cracked mirror for a while,
Till, flushed and bright-eyed, smiling a little smile,
She'd sit at the table always set for one,
To write a letter starting: "Dearest Son."

ETHEL BARNETT DE VITO

There is an enduring tenderness in the love of a mother to a son that transcends all other affections of the heart . . . she will glory in his fame and exult in his prosperity; and, if adversity overtake him, he will be the dearer to her by misfortune.

WASHINGTON IRVING

I remember she used often to look somewhat ruefully at her hands, those beautiful, useful, roughened hands of hers, so strong in the palm, so unexpectedly delicate and pointed in the fingers; not small hands, but having spare and well-shaped lines. It was always her plan that one day she would stop plunging her hands into this and that; she was going to wear gloves when she gardened and use cold cream and have really "nice" hands. She loved the white hands of ladies, the skin soft and smooth and the nails pink and tapering. But if she ever remembered to put on gloves, as sometimes once in a long time she did, sooner or later they would be off and she would be grubbing about in the earth, looking up to say apologetically, "I seem to have to feel the roots are right. They won't grow otherwise. And I do like the feel of the earth!"

PEARL BUCK

MOTHER'S LOVE

Her love is like an island
  In life's ocean, vast and wide,
A peaceful, quiet shelter
  From the wind, and rain, and tide.

'Tis bound on the north by Hope,
  By Patience on the west,
By tender Counsel on the south,
  And on the east by Rest.

Above it like a beacon light
  Shine faith, and truth, and prayer;
And through the changing scenes of life,
  I find a haven there.

ANONYMOUS

The identity wrapped up in the word *mother* may be more potent, more connotative, than meanings commonly attached to female or male, married or single, employed or unemployed, child or adult, husband or wife, rich or poor. In the psychological testing game that asks people to name the first word that comes to mind in response to certain other words, one can imagine something like the following associates: pencil — paper; car — road; book — read; food — eat; father — work; mother — home. Mother — lap. Mother — love. Mother — food. Mother — warm.

JEAN CURTIS

I cannot recall what happened during the first months after my illness. I only know that I sat in my mother's lap or clung to her dress as she went about her household duties. My hands felt every object and observed every motion, and in this way I learned to know many things. Soon I felt the need of some communication with others and began to make crude signs. A shake of the head meant "No" and a nod, "Yes," a pull meant "Come" and a push, "Go." Was it bread that I wanted? Then I would imitate the acts of cutting the slices and buttering them. If I wanted my mother to make ice cream for dinner I made the sign for working the freezer and shivered, indicating cold. My mother, moreover, succeeded in making me understand a good deal. I always knew when she wished me to bring her something, and I would run upstairs or anywhere else she indicated. Indeed, I owe to her loving wisdom all that was bright and good in my long night.

HELEN KELLER

A mother understands what a child does not say.

JEWISH PROVERB

MAMA AND HER
BANK ACCOUNT

For as long as I could remember, the small cottage on Castro Street had been home. The familiar background was there; Mama, Papa, my only brother, Nels. There was my sister Christine, closest to me in age, yet ever secret and withdrawn — and the littlest sister, Dagmar.

There, too, came the Aunts, Mama's four sisters. Aunt Jenny, who was the oldest and the bossiest; Aunt Sigrid; Aunt Marta; and our maiden Aunt Trina.

The Aunts' old bachelor uncle, my Great-Uncle Chris — the "black Norwegian" — came with his great impatience, his shouting and stamping. And brought mystery and excitement to our humdrum days.

But the first awareness was of Mama.

I remember that every Saturday night Mama would sit down by the scrubbed kitchen table and with much wrinkling of usually placid brows count out the money Papa had brought home in the little envelope.

There would be various stacks.

"For the landlord," Mama would say, piling up the big silver pieces.

"For the grocer." Another group of coins.

"For Katrin's shoes to be half-soled." And Mama would count out the little silver.

"Teacher says this week I'll need a notebook." That would be Christine or Nels or I.

Mama would solemnly detach a nickel or a dime and set it aside.

We would watch the diminishing pile with breathless interest.

At last, Papa would ask, "Is all?"

And when Mama nodded, we could relax a little and reach for schoolbooks and homework. For Mama would look up then and smile. "Is good," she'd murmur. "We do not have to go to the Bank."

It was a wonderful thing, that Bank Account of Mama's. We were all so proud of it. It gave us such a warm, secure feeling. No one else we knew had money in a big bank downtown.

I remember when the Jensens down the street were put out because they couldn't pay their rent. We children watched the big strange men carry out the furniture, took furtive notice of poor Mrs. Jensen's shamed tears, and I was choked with sudden fear. This, then, happened to people who did not have the stack of coins marked "Landlord." Might this, could this, violence happen to us?

I clutched Christine's hands. "We have a Bank Account," she reassured me calmly, and suddenly I could breathe again.

When Nels graduated from grammar school he wanted to go on to High. "Is good," Mama said, and Papa nodded approvingly.

"It will cost a little money," Nels said.

Eagerly we brought up chairs and gathered around the table. I took down the gaily painted box that Aunt Sigrid had sent us from Norway one Christmas and laid it carefully in front of Mama.

This was the "Little Bank." Not to be confused, you understand, with the big Bank downtown. The "Little Bank" was used for sudden emergencies, such as the time Christine broke her arm and had to be taken to a doctor, or when Dagmar got croup and Papa had to go to the drugstore for medicine to put into the steam kettle.

Nels had it all written out neatly. So much for carfare, for clothes, for notebooks and supplies. Mama looked at the figures for a long time. Then she counted out the money in the Little Bank. There was not enough.

She pursed her lips. "We do not," she reminded us gently, "want to have to go to the Bank."

We all shook our heads.

"I will work in Dillon's grocery after school," Nels volunteered.

Mama gave him a bright smile and laboriously wrote down a sum and added and subtracted. Papa did it in his head. He was very quick on arithmetic. "Is not enough," he said. Then he took his pipe out of his mouth and looked at it for a long time. "I give up tobacco," he said suddenly.

Mama reached across the table and touched Papa's sleeve, but she didn't say anything. Just wrote down another figure.

"I will mind the Elvington children every Friday night," I said. "Christine can help me."

We all felt very good. We had passed another milestone without having to go downtown and draw money out of Mama's Bank Account. The Little Bank was sufficient for the present.

So many things, I remember, came out of the Little Bank that year. Christine's costume for the school play, Dagmar's tonsil operation, my Girl Scout uniform. And always, in the background, was the comforting knowledge that should our efforts fail, we still had the Bank to depend upon.

Even when the Strike came, Mama would not let us worry unduly. We all worked together so that the momentous trip downtown could be postponed. It was almost like a game.

During that time Mama "helped out" at Kruper's bakery for a

big sack of only slightly stale bread and coffeecake. And as Mama said, fresh bread was not too good for a person and if you put the coffeecake into the hot oven it was nearly as nice as when first baked.

Papa washed bottles at the Castro Creamery every night and they gave him three quarts of fresh milk and all the sour milk he could carry away. Mama made fine cheese.

The day the Strike was over and Papa went back to work, I saw Mama stand a little straighter, as if to get a kink out of her back.

She looked around at us proudly. "Is *good*," she smiled. "See? We did not have to go down to the Bank."

That was twenty years ago.

Last year I sold my first story. When the check came I hurried over to Mama's and put the long green slip of paper in her lap. "For you," I said, "to put in your Bank Account."

And I noticed for the first time how old Mama and Papa looked. Papa seemed shorter, now, and Mama's wheaten braids were sheened with silver.

Mama fingered the check and looked at Papa.

"Is good," she said, and her eyes were proud.

"Tomorrow," I told her, "you must take it down to the Bank."

"You will go with me, Katrin?"

"That won't be necessary, Mama. See? I've endorsed the check to you. Just hand it to the teller, he'll deposit it to your account."

Mama looked at me. "Is no account," she said. "In all my life, I never been inside a Bank."

And when I didn't — couldn't — answer, Mama said earnestly: "Is not *good* for little ones to be afraid — to not feel secure."

KATHRYN FORBES

THE READING MOTHER

I had a Mother who read to me
Sagas of pirates who scoured the sea,
Cutlasses clenched in their yellow teeth,
"Blackbirds" stowed in the hold beneath.

I had a Mother who read me lays
Of ancient and gallant and golden days;
Stories of Marmion and Ivanhoe,
Which every boy has a right to know.

I had a Mother who read me tales
Of Gêlert the hound of the hills of Wales,
True to his trust till his tragic death,
Faithfulness blent with his final breath.

I had a Mother who read me the things
That wholesome life to the boy heart brings —
Stories that stir with an upward touch,
Oh, that each mother of boys were such!

You may have tangible wealth untold;
Caskets of jewels and coffers of gold.
Richer than I you can never be —
I had a Mother who read to me.

STRICKLAND GILLILAN

THE BOOK
OUR MOTHERS READ

We search the world for truth; we cull
The good, the pure, the beautiful,
From graven stone and written scroll,
And all old flower-fields of the soul;
And, weary seekers of the best,
We come back laden from the quest,
To find that all the sages said
Is in the Book our mothers read.

JOHN GREENLEAF WHITTIER

Into the woman's keeping is committed the destiny of the generations to come after us. In bringing up your children you mothers must remember that while it is essential to be loving and tender it is no less essential to be wise and firm. Foolishness and affection must not be treated as interchangeable terms; and besides training your sons and daughters in the softer and milder virtues, you must seek to give them those stern and hardy qualities which in after life they will surely need.

Some children will go wrong in spite of the best training; and some will go right even when their surroundings are most unfortunate . . . . Teach boys and girls alike that they are not to look forward to lives spent in avoiding difficulties; teach them that work, for themselves and also for others, is not a curse but a blessing; seek to make them happy, to make them enjoy life, but seek also to make them face life with steadfast resolution, and to do their whole duty before God and to man. Surely she who can thus train her sons and daughters is thrice fortunate among women.

THEODORE ROOSEVELT

TWO TEMPLES

A Builder builded a temple,
He wrought it with grace and skill;
Pillars and groins and arches
All fashioned to work his will.
Men said, as they saw its beauty,
"It shall never know decay;
Great is thy skill, O Builder!
Thy fame shall endure for aye."

A Mother builded a temple
With loving and infinite care,
Planning each arch with patience,
Laying each stone with prayer.
None praised her unceasing efforts,
None knew of her wondrous plan,
For the temple the Mother builded
Was unseen by the eyes of man.

Gone is the Builder's temple,
Crumpled into the dust;
Low lies each stately pillar,
Food for consuming rust.
But the temple the Mother builded
Will last while the ages roll,
For that beautiful unseen temple
Was a child's immortal soul.

HATTIE VOSE HALL

THE BARGAIN

Meg, Jo, Beth and Amy. Who can forget the four March sisters immortalized by Louisa May Alcott in Little Women. *Here Meg, as a young mother, discovers she is no match for her resourceful son Demi.*

Meg made many moral rules, and tried to keep them; but what mother was ever proof against the winning wiles, the ingenious evasions, or the tranquil audacity of the miniature men and women who so early show themselves accomplished Artful Dodgers?

"No more raisins, Demi, they'll make you sick," says Mamma to the young person, who offers his services in the kitchen with unfailing regularity on plum-pudding day.

"Me likes to be sick."

"I don't want to have you, so run away and help Daisy make pat-a-cakes."

He reluctantly departs, but his wrongs weigh upon his spirit, and by and by, when an opportunity comes to redress them, he outwits Mamma by a shrewd bargain.

"Now you have been good children, and I'll play anything you like," says Meg as she leads her assistant cooks upstairs when the pudding is safely bouncing in the pot.

"Truly, Marmar?" asks Demi.

"Yes, truly, anything you say," replies the short-sighted parent, preparing herself to sing "The Three Little Kittens" half a dozen times over, or to take her family to "Buy a penny bun," regardless of wind or limb. But Demi corners her by the cool reply: "Then we'll go and eat up all the raisins."

My mother had a great deal of trouble with me but I think she enjoyed it.

SAMUEL CLEMENS

There never was a woman like her. She was gentle as a dove and brave as a lioness . . . The memory of my mother and her teachings were after all the only capital I had to start life with, and on that capital I have made my way.

ANDREW JACKSON

My mother made a brilliant impression upon my childhood life. She shone for me like the evening star — I loved her dearly, but at a distance.

WINSTON CHURCHILL

TURNING THE TABLES

In her autobiography, On Reflection, *Helen Hayes describes the day she tried a new approach when her son Jamie was being particularly naughty.*

Jamie enraged and enchanted and eventually exhausted the rest of us . . . When (we) had Bunty Cobb MacNaughton's little boy Charles stay with us during the London Blitz, he and Jamie became minikin and manikin, monkey see, monkey do. They were inseparable. They were ganging up on the dogs, the servants, and me. Too infrequently would they go at each other, a most welcome sight.

One day, the two kids were particularly obnoxious to one of the dogs, and I, in despair, remembered something my sister-in-law Helen Bishop had told me. When she was small and the children in the house were being naughty, her mother used to gather them to her knee and say, "I have been a terrible mother. If I were a good mother, you would all be good children and wouldn't be doing all these terrible things. I've been so bad as a mother that I want you to punish me." She would then direct her plea to the ringleader.

"Hit me, Darling. No, I mean it. I deserve to be hit."

Her loving children would start whimpering. "No, no, Mother, please, we'll be good. We're *sorry!*" When she forced one of them to give her a token slap, a great wail would go up and all the imps would cling to their mother, begging for forgiveness. After they had comforted her and she them, they would go off, red-eyed and chastened.

I was absolutely touched by this charming cure; it was so creative. Jamie was racing around like an Indian, smacking (our dog) Turvey's bottom with a stick. It was in the midst of their cookie feud.

"Jamie!" I beckoned. "Come here, Darling." He and his little partner in crime cautiously approached me. I was at the pool, sitting in a low beach chair in my bathing suit.

"Don't be afraid, Jamie. I want to talk to you."

The boys stood at my side as I rested my book on my lap. I repeated the Georgianna MacArthur dialogue, ending sanctimoniously with "If you must hit someone, hit me, your wicked mother, not poor Turvey!"

Jamie pulled his ear to make sure he had heard correctly. His eyes were round with disbelief. What he usually heard was the maternal, "If you do not leave that poor animal alone, I will kick you to kingdom come."

This was all strange to Jamie — a brand-new mom. Our English house guest had all the innocence of the Artful Dodger.

"Hit her, Jamie," he encouraged my son. "Go on and hit her."

I could have slapped him.

"Yes, I deserve it, Jamie. I've been a bad mother."

It was beautiful: Jamie was rendered utterly helpless. He just stared at me.

"She told you to hit her," young MacNaughton pressed on. "Go ahead and hit her."

Jamie was roused from his reverie. He turned to his friend and then to me. I felt like Mae Marsh in *Over the Hill* — all cameo, lace dickey, and workworn-motherhood. My son picked up the stick with which he had been harassing Turvey, took a low swing, and cracked me across the shins with all his might . . .

I could never catch him. It was (his father) who got the chance to use the hairbrush.

ONE CROWDED HOUR
OF GLORIOUS STRIFE

I love my daughters with a love unfailing,
I love them healthy and I love them ailing.
I love them as sheep are loved by the shepherd,
With a fiery love like a lion or a leopard.
I love them gentle or inclined to mayhem —
But I love them warmest after eight-thirty a.m.

Oh, the peace like heaven
That wraps me around,
Say, at eight-thirty-seven,
When they're schoolroom-bound
With the last glove mated
And the last scarf tied,
With the pigtail plaited,
With the pincurl dried,
And the egg disparaged,
And the porridge sneered at,
And last night's comics furtively peered at,
The coat apprehended
On its ultimate hook,
And the cover mended
On the history book!

How affection swells, how my heart leaps up
As I sip my coffee from a lonely cup!

For placid as the purling of woodland waters
Is a house divested of its morning daughters.
Sweeter than the song of the lark in the sky
Are my darlings' voices as they shriek good-by —

With the last shoe burnished
And the last pen filled,
And the bus fare furnished
And the radio stilled;
When I've signed the excuses
And written the notes,
And poured fresh juices
Down ritual throats,
And rummaged for umbrellas
Lest the day grow damper,
And rescued homework from an upstairs hamper,
And stripped my wallet
In the daily shakedown,
And tottered to my pallet
For a nervous breakdown.

Oh, I love my daughters with a love that's reckless
As Cornelia's for the jewels in her fabled necklace.
But Cornelia, even, must have raised three cheers
At the front door closing on her school-bent dears.

PHYLLIS MCGINLEY

THE WALK

When my husband Paul comes in from the fields and misses me, the children may tell him, "Mom's gone over the hill again." This means that things at home have become more than a trifle thick and I've walked out for a spell.

I would like to be the soul of graciousness and serenity, enjoying all my work. But I am not. I am impatient with weeds, I detest doing dishes and I can be blind to a dangling cobweb for a month. If I am also exasperated about the price of hogs, I may blow up simply because small Bill and his dog break a bucketful of eggs, or because the girls have been pokey with their chores today.

Suddenly I may recall an admonition of Scripture: ". . . provoke not your children to wrath." Then I know it's time to go over the hill.

Over the hill is where the Boy Britches come first in the spring, shooting up overnight. Little Bill picked huge fistfuls one April day, and Joan taught him to say "Happy Easter, Mommy" as he presented them to me. We had ham for dinner that Sunday, and Bill's wild flowers arranged on the table.

Over the hill is where fat old frogs gossip at our pond. Once our neighbors got a gallon of frog legs there in an hour; but our delight is in the frogs' antics, not their table value. Barbara, age 14, likes to toss a pebble in their midst and watch them leap up and plunge into the water.

My hill descends to a small brook that twists along to join Big Creek. Big Creek is forbidden to the children, but here at the brook I see the dam the girls built last week. Beside it is the small corral of twigs Barb contrived to confine a young mole she captured. I've suspected Joan of tender skulduggery in connection with the mole's escape; she was that upset over Barb's plan to dissect him and study him under her microscope.

One hill leads to another. In season, that next slope has a pink and white carpet of Spring Beauty, and beyond that is a hill where we cannot walk in April without crushing blue blossoms. Bluebell Hill may soon be leveled to make a new highway. So we have a special duty. Every time one of us visits the timber, he digs up some bluebells and transplants them to the grove farther on.

Here is the hickory grove. I pat the dirt round my bluebell transplants, hoping our efforts to move a hillful of flowers will be successful. We must cut a branch of this green hickory; then at our next cookout we'll smoke up a storm in order to hickory-flavor our hot dogs.

I might as well go on to Big Creek and check the creek gaps. When water rises after a rain, debris may dash against the fence and cause a lot of damage. But all's well: in fact, some new patching on the barbed wire tells me that Neighbor Brown has been here before me . . .

Now I have come full circle, and here's home — needing me, no doubt! The young ones rush to meet me. Little Bill flings himself against me exuberantly; Joan is talking a mile a minute; Barbara's eyes shine a quiet welcome.

These are my good kids; here are the home and farm I love. How could I have been so annoyed with them only a couple of hours ago?

"Where have you been?" my husband asks. I say, "Oh, just over the hill," and the grins we exchange mean we both know that everything is pretty much right again.

MYRTLE FELKNER

NOBODY KNOWS
BUT MOTHER

How many buttons are missing today?
Nobody knows but Mother.
How many playthings are strewn in her way?
Nobody knows but Mother.
How many thimbles and spools has she missed?
How many burns on each fat little fist?
How many bumps to be cuddled and kissed?
Nobody knows but Mother.

How many hats has she hunted today?
Nobody knows but Mother.
Carelessly hiding themselves in the hay—
Nobody knows but Mother.
How many handkerchiefs wilfully strayed?
How many ribbons for each little maid?
How for her care can a mother be paid?
Nobody knows but Mother.

How many muddy shoes all in a row?
Nobody knows but Mother.
How many stockings to darn, do you know?
Nobody knows but Mother.
How many little torn aprons to mend?
How many hours of toil must she spend?
What is the time when her day's work shall end?
Nobody knows but Mother.

MARY MORRISON

LITTLE THINGS

Dear God, please give to me
A thankful heart for little things—
For sunshine on my kitchen floor,
For news the postman brings . . .

Grant me appreciation
Of small joys that are mine—
The children's birthday parties,
My honeysuckle vine;
The clean, fresh smell
Of clothes just washed;
The ivy on my wall
The children's thrilled delight
To wake and find the first snowfall.
For robins in the springtime,
And autumn's crispy weather—
For leaves that crunch;
Friends in for lunch
And laughter shared together.

. . . I do not ask contentment
That would ambition stay—
But let me love the little things
I find along the way.

HELEN LOWRIE MARSHALL

A woman who runs her house well is both its queen and its subject. She is the one who makes work possible for her husband and children, she protects them from worries, feeds them and cares for them. She is Minister of Finance, and thanks to her, the household budget is balanced. She is Minister of Fine Arts, and it is to her doing if the house or apartment has charm. She is Minister of Family Education and responsible for the boys' entry into school and college and the girls' cleverness and cultivation. A woman should be as proud of her success in making her house into a perfect little world as the greatest statesman of his in organizing a nation's affairs.

ANDRÉ MAUROIS

When there is a mother in the house, matters speed well.

AMOS BRONSON ALCOTT

THE PLEASANT WAYS
OF HOMES

I love the pleasant ways of homes,
Where time is held in gracious hands
And thoughts are shared in quietness
With someone else who understands

I love the peace of growing things,
The whispering trees, the singing birds,
And nature's simple melody
That runs too deep for human words;

The lowly tasks of every day,
The family meals, the friendly cheer,
The little daily services
That sharing makes so close and dear,

These ancient, ordered plans of life
That hedge us in along the way
But hold within their friendly hands
Some bit of glory for each day.

FRANCES MCKINNON MORTON

The mother at home quietly placing the dishes on
   the supper table,
The mother with mild words, clean her cap and
   gown, a wholesome odor falling off her
   person and clothes as she walks by . . .

WALT WHITMAN

WHEN THERE'S
LOVE AT HOME

There is beauty all around,
   When there's love at home;
There is joy in every sound,
   When there's love at home.
Peace and plenty here abide,
   Smiling sweet on every side,
Time doth softly, sweetly glide,
   When there's love at home.

JOHN H. MCNAUGHTON

MAGIC

Some women have a magic way
Of putting cheer into a room:
A swift, transforming touch that sends
The light into a shaded gloom.
They have a lovely way of giving
A cheerful, happy look to living.

A wood fire crackling on a hearth;
Old brasses rubbed and gleaming bright;
Red tulips in an earthen bowl,
The luster of worn boards scrubbed white—
Some women have a way of knowing
That household wares should be kept glowing.

I never see a woman's hands
Move swiftly at their burnishings,
But that they always seem to bear
A likeness to white flying wings:
They are so beautiful at giving
A cheerful, happy look to living.

GRACE NOLL CROWELL

LIKE MOTHER
USED TO MAKE

The other day, I read in a readers'-request column this plea:
"Can someone please tell me how to make old-fashioned apple
strudel? I have the recipe my mother used; but somehow, my
apple strudel never turns out the way hers did, and I'm won-
dering what I could be doing wrong."

Will she ever find the secret? I, too, wondered. No matter
how many readers try to help her, how many suggestions she
receives about the extra dash of sugar, the freshness of the
butter, the temperature of the oven, the timing of the baking,
will any one ever be able to reproduce the magic formula that
was her mother's, and hers alone?

Like Mother used to make . . . Bakers long have claimed the
slogan; advertisers have lured us with it to their pickles and
catsups and jellies and jams.

Like Mother used to make . . . The very words conjure up a
kitchen where a woman toils lovingly to fashion her family's
favorite dishes. It paints a nostalgic picture of children flocking
around wanting to help — to beat the eggs, to stir the batter,
to roll out the piecrust, to cut the cookies, to handle the bread
dough. It re-creates a hundred small, significant scenes — of
people who come sniffing into a kitchen, begging a taste of
this, a nibble of that, peering into the oven and pleading,
"Something smells good. Is supper ready? I'm starved."

Like Mother used to make . . . The cheese soufflé. The nut
bread. The chicken casserole. The potato pancakes. The
cherry pie. The Christmas plum pudding.

Recipes we have aplenty, passed along to daughters, presented to sons' brides. "Johnny is awfully fond of upside-down cake. I always made it this way." And eagerly the young wife follows directions, does her best to duplicate that special dish. But she knows, even when he's too polite to tell her, that something is different about it. Whatever her skills or practice, something is missing, some rare, lost ingredient that not even the best-intentioned cook can supply.

Because a mother stirs a little bit of herself into everything she cooks for her family. Unseen, all unsuspected, into the bowl goes the subtle flavor of her personality — the way she thinks and feels, the way she laughs or tilts her head or scolds. And into this dish of hers, too, go the whole measure and taste of the home — the way the dining room used to look when the lamps were lighted, the sound of family voices, the laughter, the quarrels, the memories.

These are the ingredients we lack when we try to reproduce the dish that Mother used to make. These are her secret spices. They are not for sale, and they can't be passed along.

Yet every woman who enters a kitchen carries with her a rare and precious store of her own. The flavor of *herself* in relation to her children; the warmth and tang and savor of her own household. Daily, inescapably, without ever realizing it, all of us are blending these inimitable components into other dishes, into other lives.

So that one day our children, too, will say, "My mother used to make the most wonderful peach cobbler. I simply can't make it come out the same, no matter how hard I try!"

MARJORIE HOLMES

MOTHER KNEADING DOUGH

She shapes the supple, pliant dough
With apt and dexterous hands, that know
By some untaught, unerring touch
The perfect pressure, neither much
Nor little, that makes each fluffy, light
Roll, and each crusty loaf, a sight
To rest the eye and ease the mind
With something comforting and kind,
As if each rounded form were blent
To shape and substance of content.

She has no art for shaping love
To words men know the meaning of,
So molds with deft and gentle hand
The forms that all can understand,
And those who eat her loaves are fed
With more than baking, more than bread.

JANE MERCHANT

OLD RECIPE BOOK

This brings my Mother closer to me now
Than pen or portrait — just this faded book.
Only ingredients are listed here: not how
To mix them. I can see her reproachful look:
"Why, you remember that, my child, for certain!"
I can hear her saying: "That one is from Mabel!"
I recall sun shifting through a gingham curtain
Making a stained-glass cover for the table.
I use these recipes now over and over:
Fat biscuit, shortcake, and top-heavy loaves
Of golden-crusted bread as sweet as clover,
And when the scent of cinnamon and cloves
Spice the warm air, those days return once more,
And memory consecrates each homely chore.

ELEANOR ALLETTA CHAFFEE

She broke the bread into two fragments, and gave them to the children, who ate with avidity. "She hath kept none for herself," grumbled the Sergeant. "Because she is not hungry," said a soldier. "Because she is a mother," said the Sergeant.

VICTOR HUGO

I can still smell the warm spicy smells of gingersnaps baking in the oven, of apple pies rich with cinnamon, and of countless doughnuts merrily bobbing about on the surface of boiling fat. My mother sang hymns as she went about her work and often encouraged us to sing with her. One of her favorites was "Shall we gather at the River?" and all of us, joining in the chorus, loved to assure her that we would most certainly gather there. "Yes, we'll gather at the river, the beautiful river, the beautiful river," we would all shout together, each, I feel sure, thinking of that river only as some pleasant family picnicking ground on some pleasant undefined day in the future.

MARY ELLEN CHASE

A mother is a mother still,
The holiest thing alive.

S. T. COLERIDGE

Children are the anchors that hold a mother to life.

SOPHOCLES

. . . Never was a woman more richly mother than this woman, bubbling over with a hundred little songs and scraps of gay nonsense to beguile a child from tears, and filled with wayward moods as she was, yet her hands were swift to tenderness and care and quiet brooding tending when need arose. Never was she a more perfect mother than during the summers on the mountain top when she could give herself freely to her children. She led them here and there in search of beauty, and she taught them to love cliffs and rugged rocks outlined against the sky, and to love also little dells where ferns and moss grow about a pool. Beauty she brought into her house too and filled the rooms with ferns and flowers.

PEARL BUCK

THE DAY WE FLEW
THE KITES

A wise mother reminds her child of the sheer joy of living.

"String!" shouted Brother, bursting into the kitchen. "We need lots more string."

It was Saturday. As always, it was a busy one, for "Six days shalt thou labor and do all thy work" was taken seriously then. Outside, Father and Mr. Patrick next door were doing chores.

Inside the two houses, Mother and Mrs. Patrick were engaged in spring cleaning. Such a windy March day was ideal for "turning out" clothes closets. Already woolens flapped on back-yard clotheslines.

Somehow the boys had slipped away to the back lot with their kites. Now, even at the risk of having Brother impounded to beat carpets, they had sent him for more string. Apparently there was no limit to the heights to which kites would soar today.

My mother looked out the window. The sky was piercingly blue; the breeze fresh and exciting. Up in all that blueness sailed puffy billows of clouds. It had been a long, hard winter, but today was Spring.

Mother looked at the sitting room, its furniture disordered for a Spartan sweeping. Again her eyes wavered toward the window. "Come on, girls! Let's take string to the boys and watch them fly the kites a minute." On the way we met Mrs. Patrick, laughing guiltily, escorted by her girls.

There never was such a day for flying kites! God doesn't make two such days in a century. We played all our fresh twine into the boys' kites and still they soared. We could hardly distinguish the tiny, orange-colored specks. Now and then we slowly reeled one in, finally bringing it dipping and tugging to earth, for the sheer joy of sending it up again. What a thrill to run with them, to the right, to the left, and see our poor, earthbound movements reflected minutes later in the majestic sky-dance of the kites! We wrote wishes on slips of paper and slipped them over the string. Slowly, irresistibly, they climbed up until they reached the kites. Surely all such wishes would be granted!

Even our fathers dropped hoe and hammer and joined us. Our mothers took their turn, laughing like schoolgirls. Their hair blew out of the pompadours and curled loose about their cheeks; their gingham aprons whipped about their legs. Mingled with our fun was something akin to awe. The grownups were really playing with us! Once I looked at Mother and thought she looked actually pretty. And her over forty!

We never knew where the hours went on that hilltop day. There were no hours, just a golden, breezy Now. I think we were all a little beyond ourselves. Parents forgot their duty and their dignity; children forgot their combativeness and small spites. "Perhaps it's like this in the Kingdom of Heaven," I thought confusedly.

It was growing dark before, drunk with sun and air, we all stumbled sleepily back to the houses. I suppose we had some sort of supper. I suppose there must have been a surface tidying-up, for the house on Sunday looked decorous enough.

The strange thing was, we didn't mention that day afterward. I felt a little embarrassed. Surely none of the others had thrilled to it as deeply as I. I locked the memory up in that deepest part of me where we keep "the things that cannot be and yet are."

The years went on, then one day I was scurrying about my own kitchen in a city apartment, trying to get some work out of the way while my three-year-old insistently cried her desire to "go park and see ducks."

"I *can't* go!" I said. "I have this and this to do, and when I'm through I'll be too tired to walk that far."

My mother, who was visiting us, looked up from the peas she was shelling. "It's a wonderful day," she offered; "really warm, yet there's a fine, fresh breeze. It reminds me of that day we flew the kites."

I stopped in my dash between stove and sink. The locked door flew open, and with it a gush of memories. I pulled off my apron. "Come on," I told my little girl. "You're right, it's too good a day to miss."

FRANCES FOWLER

PHILOSOPHY FOR MOTHERS

When he grows up, I don't think he'll recall
How, on a sapphire morning in the fall,
Dust pussies tumbled up and down the stair,
And smudges lined the woodwork here and there,
While he and I ran hand in hand together,
Carefree, into the bright October weather.

I hope my son looks back upon today
And sees a mother who had time to play
Whether the work was done, or it was not;
Who realized chores are sometimes best forgot.
There will be years for cleaning house and cooking,
But little boys grow up when we're not looking.

BARBARA OVERTON CHRISTIE

TO MY MOTHER

"When I grow up," I had always said,
Squaring my shoulders and shaking my head,
"I'll do whatever I want to do. . . ."
But I always came back for a kiss from you.
When I grew up I was somewhat stern
And wondered if you would ever learn
That I was adult and therefore wise
But I leaned on the love in your steady eyes.
With what true thread of wisdom and dream
You mended the sails and stitched the seam
Of my wayward craft, I cannot know;
I can only write as the swift years go
With the tides of time, we have shared together
A lovely mother-and-daughter weather
And kept in balance a sweet and fine
Ebb and flow of your heart and mine.

GLADYS MCKEE

DAYS WHEN
I AM SEWING

A thousand things remind us of our mothers —
But days when I am sewing you return
Most easily: in the mystery of laying
A tissue pattern out to best advantage,
In the scissors' clean bite of the crispy goods,
The basting (thank you for insisting on it),
The stitching, and the ultimate delight
Of seeing garments grow to perfect fit.

Some mothers come back best in poetry
Or music, or good laughter, or in gardens —
But, days when I am sewing, I admit
I never can be certain whether my
Hands happily repeat the tricks you taught,
Or these are your hands, come alive in me.

ELAINE V. EMANS

SHARED MOMENTS

Judith Viorst recounts the pleasures and bittersweet moments of motherhood.

My eight-year-old son, Alexander, and I sit on the floor in the living room. We're sewing. I'm putting patches on jeans. He's putting seams in some purple felt, which he's making into a drawstring purse for his grandma. A wave of contentment sweeps over me. "It's nice," I softly say. "It's nice to be sitting here sewing with my boy." And this dirty-faced thug with the matted hair looks up at me and smiles. "It's nice," he says, "to be sewing with my mommy."

The raising of our consciousness within the past ten years has shaken up our old-time notions of motherhood, and most of the people I know would never insist these days that all real women want babies, that motherhood is always deeply fulfilling, that other, nonmotherhood paths to personal growth and satisfaction can't be as good as having a child. In the process, however, of stating the case against the glorification of being a mother, it sometimes is made to seem like a sentence to hell. So while we're re-examining what's foolish and coercive in many of our mindless motherhood myths, I'd like to take time out to speak of some of motherhood's very special pleasures.

The foremost of these pleasures is the pleasure, for me, of an intimate love relationship, which, if I were forced to choose, I'd choose over wisdom and wealth and a Nobel prize. Happiness is hanging around with people I really know and really care about, which doesn't have to mean — as my friend Joanne points out — that when kindergarten is closed on account of snow and we get to have our children home all day, we're crazy about it.

What I *am* crazy about, however, is the intensity of our involvement with one another and the power we have to give meaning and weight and sometimes even beauty to the shared experience of daily life. "Music I heard with you was more than music, and bread I broke with you was more than bread" is how a poem I love a lot describes it. Or, as a friend's little girl once explained while taking a walk with her mother one chill winter day: "It doesn't feel so cold when there's someone to walk with."

Another pleasure of motherhood is being so thoroughly needed and so depended upon, of being so fiercely important to some other life, of being — in the eyes of these particular human beings — their One and Only, Indispensable Mommy. The mommy who puts on the Band-Aids. The mommy who butters the bread. The mommy in "I want Mommy" and "Mommy's home." The mommy who's expected to get off the phone and out of the shower and stop making dinner or love when her kid starts to cry. The mommy who knows it's impossible to glue back the ear on the bunny but who's expected to try.

There's also joy in the opposite — in watching something grow, even though part of that growing is away from us, and even though we aren't quite as glad as we thought we would be about getting phased out of those lace-up-my-shoelaces jobs. "I can carry the suitcase, Mommy — I'm a big boy now," is, for me, precisely the meaning of "bittersweet." Yet, watching our kids wave a jaunty goodby and go striding off down the street on the sturdy and confident legs that perhaps we helped give them provides us with (in addition to the funny lump in our throats) enormous pleasure.

When counting the pleasures of motherhood I also must include the pleasure of sharing the world from a child's point of view, of being let in on their fantasies, their discoveries, their delicious misconceptions.

A child's point of view can be shockingly blunt and shamelessly self-absorbed and often unintentionally hilarious, and often (when we've finished laughing at it) stunningly true. Listen to my youngest son, quite earnestly explaining why being a kid is better than being grown up:

"First," he said, "we don't have to go to dinner parties.

"And second of all," he said, "we get to climb trees.

"And third," was his callous conclusion, "we get to live longer."

Sharing a child's perspective, in addition to making us laugh, can sometimes renew and revive our lost sense of wonder, reminding us that waterfalls and peanuts and giraffes are really quite remarkable creations. Said one little girl to her mother, having very carefully looked at a butterfly, "What a good idea!" Said the little girl's mother to me, "You know, she's right."

Many mothers say that it is only with their children that they fully make another's joy their own — that partaking in the pleasure of their children is itself a pleasure too. And while such statements run the risk of sounding too, too saintly, I understand exactly what they mean. For when we watch a child of ours overcome with bliss while gazing at a just-what-he-wanted present, or trotting around in a pair of shiny new boots, or finally getting the basketball in the basket, or figuring out that c-a-t spells *cat*, what we sometimes actually feel is not happy *for* him but happy *with* him, as if, indeed, his happiness belonged to us, as if it were very directly and deeply our own.

MOTHER

I think it was a girlish hand,
    Unlined, well tended, when it held
At first, my clinging baby hand
    In gentle grasp by love impelled.

I think it was a youthful face
    That bent above me as I lay
Asleep, and bright the eyes that watched
    My rest, in that forgotten day.

I think it was a slender form
    That bore my weight on tiring arm,
And swift young feet that watched my steps
    To guide them from the ways of harm.

But years and cares have changed that form
    And face and hand; have streaked with gray
The hair; yet is the heart as full
    Of love as in that other day.

And she has her reward; not fame,
    Or baubles bought in any mart,
But motherhood's brave crown, the love
    And homage of her own child's heart.

CLARA AIKEN SPEER

As I did two smash hits with Harold Rome — *Wish You Were Here* and *Fanny* — at one point I met his mother. I poured out my enthusiasm for his lyrics and particularly for his musical talent.

She listened, smiling, and then said quietly, "I sang all those tunes into his ear when he was a baby."

JOSH LOGAN

MOMMA

Metropolitan Opera star Robert Merrill's mother dreamed of the day her son would become an opera singer. Here he describes the day her dream also became his.

It is true that my mother knew I was going to be a singer before I ever dreamt it. But I remember exactly how our ambitions became one, and the exact moment.

My jobs were so short-lived and so numerous that I don't remember whether I was working for Good Health Seltzer, Ideal Toy, or a ladies'-belts factory. But no matter where I worked, I never missed a singing lesson. Although I still wouldn't sing for anybody but my buddies out on Coney Island or in Lincoln Terrace Park, my time with Mr. Margolis had improved my voice. It was growing stronger, clearer, easier.

One day Momma met me at the studio. She was unbelievable. It wasn't enough that Mr. Margolis was teaching me without a fee, she now wanted something else.

"Mr. Margolis — mine boy, is doing all right?"

"I'm quite pleased, Mrs. Miller, with his progress. I am starting to give him some Stradella."

"Stra . . ."

"He's an Italian composer who wrote long before Verdi or even Mozart. Seventeenth century. Alessandro Stradella! His work is very florid, very colorful, exciting."

"It can stretch the voice, take it new places?"

"That's right, Mrs. Miller," my teacher said in awe.

"Moishe's lucky to have you, Mr. Margolis. I mean *Morris*, my singer of the Italian seventeenth century. I feel nothing but good from this."

She now grabbed my earlobes and pulled them. "So nothing will *beshrie* mine boy," she explained.

"I understand, Mrs. Miller."

"The boy has never heard opera — the whole thing. Isn't it good for him to hear an opera?"

"Very good."

She pointed at his wall, filled with the autographed pictures of singer friends and pupils. "Mr. Margolis! Through a friend, maybe Mr. Martinelli up there, you can get us free tickets some night — or the cheapest? Only, even the cheapest we can't afford so good. We can sit anywhere, who cares?"

I was embarrassed. Mr. Margolis was doing so much already. "Momma, Mr. Margolis is too busy t-t-to . . ."

"I talked to you? Is your name changed again? First Moishe, then Morris, now Margolis?"

My teacher laughed. "I will try. It's a good idea, Mrs. Miller."

"Thank you. You see, it wasn't such a calamity my asking. Mr. Martinelli is singing a lot this week. I was reading the program."

My mother was all *chutzpah* — the ultimate in nerve. Nothing ever bothered her, no obstacle ever made her hesitate. Why should the great Martinelli give us tickets? I was mortified by her request, but not so much that I refused to go a few nights later when Mr. Margolis managed to get three tickets to *Il Trovatore*. I never saw Momma so excited. Three nights after Momma had wangled the invitation, Mr. Margolis led us to the upper plate, the Family Circle, the highest point of the Opera House — so near the ceiling that I found myself reminded of Lon Chaney's *The Phantom of the Opera*, the climax of which was the crashing of the great chandelier . . .

The curtain parted on the entrance to the Count di Luna's palace. Mr. Margolis had told us the story of *Il Trovatore* — an almost impossible task — and now I watched in fascination as the confusing tale unfolded.

It was Richard Bonelli as Count di Luna who altered my life forever. I was impressed beyond belief — stunned by him. That night Richard Bonelli changed me from a confused stage-struck kid to a true opera student.

The elevator was so crowded that we quietly spiraled down the stairs, leaving the theater in a daze. After we thanked Mr. Margolis and said good night, Momma and I started for the subway.

We sat rereading our programs as the train jogged along to Brooklyn. I looked up from my program at my mother's strong and beautiful profile.

When I spoke, there wasn't a trace of a stutter in my voice. "I want that, Momma. *That's* what I want," I repeated, to make certain all the facts were in.

My mother never even looked up from her program. "That's good, Moishe. I'm glad."

She seemed to have no idea of the revolution that had taken place inside me. It never occurred to me that she had prepared the way for revolution and was not in the least surprised now that all her plots had begun to thicken. As far as she was concerned, I had just picked up the option on that contract she and I had all my life.

"I'm glad, Moishe," she now repeated. "So tell me — why? What makes you so sure now?"

What could I say? I was filled to brimming. A completely new feeling carried me away. "I just know I can sing louder than Bonelli," I said.

JOE WILLIE'S ROSE

In his autobiography with Dick Schaap, I Can't Wait Until Tomorrow . . . 'Cause I Get Better Looking Every Day, *Joe Willie Namath pays tribute to his mother.*

My mother — her name is Rose Szolnoki now — raised me, and she had her hands full. I think she did a helluva job. She taught me to be polite and to respect my elders. She's a great lady, and she loves to talk. She talks very slowly and very properly. We have a running gag among my friends that whenever my mother calls on the phone she uses up the first three minutes just to say hello. And she does some of the funniest things in the world. When she watches the Jets play on television, she prays to two saints, one when we've got the ball and one when the other team's got the ball. She's the only person I know who has an offensive and a defensive saint.

MY MOTHER

They say the most of mothers
    Are something pretty fine,
But nobody else's mother
    Can be so dear as mine.

She never fails or falters
    When things go hard or wrong;
No matter what my troubles,
    She'll help me right along.

Her thought for me is endless —
    A million times a day
She gives me love and comfort,
    For which I cannot pay.

I can't begin to tell her
    My love in just a line,
But no one else's mother
    Is quite so dear as mine.

BARBARA WHITE

When the oath of office had been administered, and President James A. Garfield had reverently kissed the Bible and sealed his compact with the nation to rightly administer its law for the term for which he was chosen, when thousands of eyes rested upon him to see the next act in the drama being enacted, in the presence of the foreign dignitaries and leading men of the country, he turned to his aged mother, who had been unconsciously weeping during the delivery of his address, and kissed her; then he kissed his wife — the two persons of all the world most interested with him in the events they had witnessed.

The act, the most unexpected at that moment, called forth cheers from the multitude who witnessed it, and the one incident of the inauguration that most impressed upon all who saw it was the tribute paid to his mother and wife by the President. Wherever the soldiers wandered in Washington during that day, wherever the news was flashed over the wires to the distant sections of our own country or to foreign lands, was heard this sentence: "The President kissed his mother."

LAURA C. HOLLOWAY

All that I am my mother made me.

JOHN QUINCY ADAMS

Most of all the other beautiful things in life come by twos and threes, by dozens and hundreds. Plenty of roses, stars, sunsets, rainbows, brothers and sisters, aunts and cousins, but only one mother in the whole world.

KATE DOUGLAS WIGGIN

There's a silvery whiteness that runs through her hair and a softness you'd like to caress. The white is the growth from the purity there and the soft from her heartbeats, I guess.

I often have thoughtfully gazed in her eyes and I've known of the message that's told. Sincerity really makes a man realize that it's love and affection they hold.

I've had her advice since the day I was born and she's taught me what's wrong and what's right. She cheers me whenever I'm feeling forlorn and she makes all my dark days seem bright.

More wondrous, by far, than the fortunes of gold that some time may cross o'er my palm. It's been my good fortune to have and to hold the sweetheart I've always called Mom.

So, I'll tell the world that I'm proud as can be of this best friend I ever have had. If she can just feel half that proudness for me, I'll have reason enough to feel glad.

HAL COCHRANE

A HEART SO LARGE

*In recalling this episode from his childhood, Mark Twain paints
for us a vivid picture of his brave and compassionate mother.*

Technically speaking, she had no career; but she had a charac-
ter and it was of a fine and striking and lovable sort. . . .

She had a slender, small body but a large heart — a heart so
large that everybody's grief and everybody's joys found welcome in it and hospitable accommodation. The greatest
difference which I find between her and the rest of the people
whom I have known is this, and it is a remarkable one: those
others felt a strong interest in a few things, whereas to the very
day of her death she felt a strong interest in the whole world
and everything and everybody in it. In all her life she never
knew such a thing as a halfhearted interest in affairs and people, or an interest which drew a line and left out certain affairs
and was indifferent to certain people. The invalid who takes a
strenuous and indestructible interest in everything and everybody but himself, and to whom a dull moment is an unknown
thing and an impossibility, is a formidable adversary for disease
and a hard invalid to vanquish. I am certain that it was this
feature of my mother's make-up that carried her so far toward
ninety.

Her interest in people and other animals was warm, personal, friendly. She always found something to excuse, and as
a rule to love, in the toughest of them — even if she had to put

it there herself. She was the natural ally and friend of the friendless. . . .

When her pity or her indignation was stirred by hurt or shame inflicted upon some defenseless person or creature, she was the most eloquent person I have heard speak. It was seldom eloquence of a fiery or violent sort, but gentle, pitying, persuasive, appealing; and so genuine and nobly and simply worded and so touchingly uttered, that many times I have seen it win the reluctant and spendid applause of tears. Whenever anybody or any creature was being oppressed, the fears that belonged to her sex and her small stature retired to the rear and her soldierly qualities came promptly to the front. One day in our village I saw a vicious devil of a Corsican, a common terror in the town, chasing his grown daughter past cautious male citizens with a heavy rope in his hand and declaring he would wear it out on her. My mother spread her door wide to the refugee and then, instead of closing and locking it after her, stood in it and stretched her arms across it, barring the way. The man swore, cursed, threatened her with his rope; but she did not flinch or show any sign of fear; she only stood straight and fine and lashed him, shamed him, derided him, defied him in tones not audible to the middle of the street but audible to the man's conscience and dormant manhood; and he asked her pardon and gave her his rope and said with a most great and blasphemous oath that she was the bravest woman he ever saw; and so went his way without another word and troubled her no more. He and she were always good friends after that, for in her he had found a long-felt want — somebody who was not afraid of him.

MY MOTHER'S GARDEN

Her heart is like her garden,
Old-fashioned, quaint and sweet,
With here a wealth of blossoms,
And there a still retreat.
Sweet violets are hiding,
We know as we pass by,
And lilies, pure as angel thoughts,
Are opening somewhere nigh.

Forget-me-nots there linger,
To full perfection brought,
And there bloom purple pansies
In many a tender thought.
There love's own roses blossom,
As from enchanted ground,
And lavish perfume exquisite
The whole glad year around.

And in that quiet garden —
The garden of her heart —
Songbirds are always singing
Their songs of cheer apart.

ALICE E. ALLEN

THE MOTHER IN THE HOUSE

For such as you, I do believe,
Spirits their softest carpets weave,
And spread them out with gracious hand
Wherever you walk, wherever you stand.

For such as you, of scent and dew
Spirits their rarest nectar brew,
And where you sit and where you sup
Pour beauty's elixir in your cup.

For all day long, like other folk,
You bear the burden, wear the yoke,
And yet when I look in your eyes at eve
You are lovelier than ever, I do believe.

HERMANN HAGEDORN

WHAT IS A MOTHER?

A mother is a person who is old enough to be an authority on Indian war whoops and whether cowboys ever went barefoot, and yet young enough to remember the rules of the game May I? and the second verse of Sing a Song of Sixpence.

She must be smart enough to answer questions about thunder and locomotives and stars, but ignorant enough to laugh at the reason a chicken runs across the road.

She must be a detective and able to find the top to the cereal box which was thrown away last week, the treads to Greg's toy tank, and the other roller skate.

She must be a veterinarian and accomplished at taking ticks off the dog, feeding the kittens, and remembering to change the water in the goldfish bowl.

A mother must not just be a cook, proficient at cooking roasts, biscuits, chicken gravy, Mike's favorite sukiyaki and Greg's favorite spaghetti; but also must be able to decorate birthday cakes and place exactly right the raisin eyes in gingerbread men.

She must be a judge and arbitrator when someone would not let someone ride his tricycle; must be a stern disciplinarian when it comes to too much chewing gum and getting three little boys to bed at night; and she must have a well-padded shoulder for tears and comfort when his best chum throws sand at Mike and goes off with a new friend.

She must not only be an expert laundress, but always remember to remove sand and pebbles and string from pockets; and she must be a seamstress and adept at sewing on buttons, letting down and taking up sleeves and pants legs and able to patch threadbare corduroy knees so the patches do not show.

She must be a doctor and able to remove splinters without hurting, stop bleeding noses, vaporize colds, read stories to measle-speckled boys, and always have on hand an endless supply of ready-cut bandages.

A mother must also be a naturalist and able to dissect caterpillars, remove taillights from fireflies, and touch squirmy worms.

A mother must be a financial wizard and always able to stretch a meager weekly budget to include new shoes for Brian and a birthday present for someone she did not know had invited her sons to a party.

She must be a magician and keep a bottomless cooky jar, a constant supply of apples in the refrigerator, and be able instantly to recognize a scribbled drawing as a beautiful picture of a man walking down a dirt road with a pan on his head.

She must be able to balance a baby under one arm, a small boy climbing up her back and another trying to tie her feet into knots, and still write a check for the dry cleaners.

Regardless of her shape or stature, when she sits down a mother must have a lap large enough to hold three wiggling pajama-clad boys who listen wonder-eyed to "Once upon a time" stories of the world about them.

Her sense of beauty must be able to stoop low enough to see the lovely ferny plant Greg found growing under a toadstool; and must be able to stretch on tallest tiptoes to hold Mike to see the heavenly blue of the robin's egg in the nest in the sycamore tree.

A mother is a queer sort of person. In a single instant her endless cooking and dishwashing and ironing and sock darning and knee bandaging can swell over into a heart-thrilling wave of pride on visitors' day at the kindergarten when Mike stands up in his new red sweater, replies "Yes, ma'am" to the teacher, and solemnly walks to the front of the room to direct the rhythm band.

A mother's payment is rich and full, but often comes in little ways: a wadded bouquet of dandelion puffs; seeing Greg, unnoticed, share his tricycle with the new little boy across the street; watching Brian reach to pluck a neighbor's prize tulip . . . hold his hand in mid-air a second . . . and then toddle off to chase a butterfly. Her payment comes in the cherished words of a small boy's prayers at night when Mike adds a P.S. to God to "also bless Billy even though he pushed me off the swing today."

Then a mother kisses three blond heads, turns off the light and hugs a smile to her heart as she walks downstairs. And after the dishes are done, before she gets out her mending box, she puts a batch of cookies in the oven for a surprise tomorrow.

NAN CARROLL

Acknowledgments

The editor and the publisher have made every effort to trace the ownership of all copyrighted material and to secure permission from copyright holders of such material. In the event of any question arising as to the use of any material the publisher and editor, while expressing regret for inadvertent error, will be pleased to make the necessary corrections in future printings. Thanks are due to the following authors, publishers, publications and agents for permission to use the material indicated.

ABINGDON PRESS, for "New Mother's Song" from *Petals Of Light* by Jane Merchant. Copyright © 1958 by Abingdon Press.

AIRMONT PUBLISHING CO., for "Story Of My Life" from *The Story Of My Life* by Helen Keller. Copyright © 1965 by Airmont Publishing Co.

ATHENEUM PUBLISHERS, for an excerpt from *The Children* by Jan de Hartog. Copyright © 1968 by Marjorie M. de Hartog and Alan U. Schwartz, Trustees.

AL CAPP, for "Mother And Her Secret" by Al Capp condensed from Monitor, an NBC-Radio Broadcast. Copyright © 1964 by Al Capp.

DELACORTE PRESS, for an excerpt from *JOSH My Up and Down, In And Out Life* by Joshua Logan. Copyright © 1976 by Joshua L. Logan.

DOUBLEDAY & COMPANY, INC., for "Mother = Love" from *Working Mothers* by Jean Curtis. Copyright © 1975, 1976 by Jean Curtis; for "The Big Surprise" from *Love And Laughter* by Marjorie Holmes. Copyright © 1959, 1967 by Marjorie Holmes Mighell; for "Little Things" from *Bright Horizons* by Helen Lowrie Marshall. Copyright © 1954 by Helen Lowrie Marshall; for "Nobody Knows But Mother" by Mary Morrison from *The Best Loved Poems Of The American People* edited by Hazel Felleman. Copyright © 1936 by Doubleday & Company, Inc.

ELAINE V. EMANS MARSHALL and ENSIGN MAGAZINE for "Days When I Am Sewing" by Elaine V. Emans from *The Improvement Era.* Copyright © 1964 by The Church of Jesus Christ of Latter-Day Saints Church Magazines.

M. EVANS AND COMPANY, INC., for "Turning The Tables" from *On Reflection, An Autobiography* by Helen Hayes with Sanford Dody. Copyright © 1968 by Helen Hayes and Sanford Dody.

FARM JOURNAL, INC., for "Philosophy For Mothers" by Barbara Overton Christie from *Who Tells The Crocuses It's Spring?* Copyright © 1971 by Farm Journal, Inc.

HARCOURT BRACE JOVANOVICH, INC., for an excerpt from *Mama's Bank Account* by Kathryn Forbes. Copyright © 1943 by Kathryn Forbes, copyright © renewed 1971 by Richard E. McLean and Robert M. McLean.

Designed and illustrated by Betsy Beach
Set in Weiss and Weiss Italic